It Is Fun to

By Liza Charlesworth

No part of this publication can be reproduced in whole or in part, or stored in a retrieval system, or transmitted in any form or by any means, electronic, mechanical, photocopying, recording, or otherwise, without written permission of the publisher. For permission, write to Scholastic Inc.,557 Broadway, New York, NY 10012.

ISBN: 978-1-339-02673-2

Art Director: Tannaz Fassihi; Designer: Tanya Chernyak
Photos © Getty Images.
Copyright © Liza Charlesworth. All rights reserved. Published by Scholastic Inc.

3 4 5 6 7 8 9 10   68   32 31 30 29 28 27 26 25 24

Printed in Jiaxing, China. First printing, August 2023.

■ SCHOLASTIC

Camp, camp, camp!
It is fun to camp.

Grab a cap, belt, and pants.
Pack a lamp and a snack.

Set up a tent on soft grass.
Camp on the land!

You can trek past plants.
You can spot a nest
and a skunk.

You can jump in a pond.

You can drift on a raft.

You can get in the tent
and rest. Zzzzzzzzzzzz!

Is it fun to camp?
Yes, it is a blast!